ILLUSION OF BEING

COLLECTION OF POEMS

ANAMIKA MITRA

INDIA · SINGAPORE · MALAYSIA

ISBN
Paperback 979-8-89632-403-4
Hardcase 979-8-89632-809-4

In loving memory of my father
Lt. Sushil Chandra Mitra

Contents

Foreword

Though I am writing this foreword for a friend I must say that I have to look backwards and why I say so would be much clearer once we go through what Anamika is trying to tell us in her writings. This must come from someone who has profoundly seen life. This makes me tell, as, we all know that there cannot be a more exciting journey than LIFE in itself.

This pendulum of life with its troughs and crests make us and break us but very few of us takes the time out to note it down. This is important as these notes would be seen as an experience other than the writer herself and have made her vision broader at a younger age.

As it is said, habit is the second nature, I have seen Anamika writing her experiences beautifully in different forms of expressions be it a poem, a newspaper article, jounals contributions or haiku and that makes her unique.

I am privileged to write this message for her, whom I know as a scholarly attributed individual with sharp observance and courage or desire to pen down her vivid experiences.

I hope that she will continue doing this as this may be just a beginning.

Amitav Chakraborty (Author – Transient, A Temporary Abode)

(Ex IAF/Ex ACSs)

15.11.2024

Introduction

Illusion of Being

Collection of Poems

This collection of poems is nothing more than life experiences sprinkled with imagination where reality couldn't stretch. Not every aspect of life that we live through is actually happening and real. Some are fragments of imagination and abstract thinking which might be blurred with the passage of time. But we live in momentary truthfulness and the best part of it is – neither the moment stays nor is truthfulness perfected. Yet we believe in what we live through without much thought to perceive otherwise and think differently. Hence, the poems are shaped out of life's experiences and encounters. Yet the whole of it is somewhere blurred and those are the areas where imagination finished the verse and spiced things up to complete and give meaning to the poems.

The poems are categorised as – Thoughtful, Feelings, Existence and Ethereal. Some poems may feel like being categorised wrongly but that is the essence of this collection. Nothing is permanent beyond that very moment in which it is created. Experiences and understanding may overlap and criss-cross over a span of time. This is done so as to make understand the extent of illusion that we each are part of in the course of our being alive.

Firstly, I pay homage to my dear father, Lt. Sushil Chandra Mitra, whose deep understanding of life and its practicalities have shaped my persona and made me able to take up challenges to the extent of again penning down few lines for my dear readers.

I am thankful to my mother who patiently bears with my absent presence in her life even though we share the same roof (I assume I live in the illusion of being busy always). Her perseverance has shown me the extent of the indomitable spirit of a woman.

I share my thankfulness and love to my children Atisha Mitra and Manavendra Mitra who in spite of their tender age have been constantly pushing me to achieve and accomplish. However, as a mother I wish them the same in multiple folds.

I would express my heartfelt gratitude to Amitav Chakraborty whose friendship has stood the test of time and who has humbly penned the foreword for 'Illusion of Being – Collection of Poems'.

I am very thankful to the team of Notion Press whose professional guidance has made the publication of these poems possible.

Anamika Mitra

11.11.2024

Thoughtful

Life on the Tracks

Life on the tracks
One of pleasure
Other of pain

The journey in compartments
Detached yet linked
For as long as it can stretch

Starts with a whistle
Like a baby born into the world
And the journey begins

Over a period amidst many places
It continues on the tracks
Life's experiences through passion

The stages in life
Revealed in compartments
Each with a tale to tell
Of events lived
And memories made

But the journey continues
On the tracks
To deviate is to derail
The balance is full
No matter if life is free or bonded

But life goes on
With speed and slowness
Pausing at the signals
To ponder on the journey past and ahead

The journey in compartments
Reaches its halt
In the station where life takes its call
The last wagon differently designed

Life is on the tracks
Of pleasure and pain
A journey timed
From one station to the next
In the slot of the timezone.

2022

Longings of the Mortal Soul

Yearned for life to bear
Burden that was too heavy
Responsibility that was extreme

But this longing to put through
To carry with lightness
To perform with perfection

Ordained and destined
In the pathway of life
Will come to stay

Fulfillment of desire
To be immortalized in words
To be remembered through actions
In the mortal existence.

2022

Nothingness

On the expanse of time
Everything shall fly and flow
Carried by angels
Devoured by demons

On the stretch of time
Everything shall appear and be gone
Blessed by angels
Cursed by demons

On the span of time
Nothing exists
Nor shall exist
Its nothingness.

2022

Clouds Will Carry Me

Look up
We are under the same sky
Blanketing us together
Oblivious of all things otherwise

The stars carry my kisses for you
If you can count this lifetime
For they are forever
Innumerable and unending
When the day ends
Night befalls
And we are alone and silent
The stars shall shower you with my kisses
And you shall glitter and glow
In the momentous peace
That love begets

The moon shall embrace you for me
My hugs for you
Is assigned to the moon

Always when you return tired and forlorn
The moon shall soothe your mind
Bring you home to rest and relax
In the softness of moonlight

The clouds are our pillow
Where we shall play
For its been always there
Between the two of us
For as long a time
That we are unaware of
For time indefinite
We shall never know

The clouds will carry me to you
Now in a distant land
Soon it will
Not be far away
The clouds will carry me to you
And the sky shall blanket us

Look up
We are under the same sky
Which bears a witness
Which holds our secrets

Our fears and strengths
Our wishes and dreams
Oblivious of all things otherwise.

2002

Waiting for Another Day

The morning brightness
Glows like embers
To spread light and warmth
As the sun rises
It befalls on each element
And you too shall not be spared

You will glow
In shades of coyness
As the day opens up
And you still can't leave the embrace
Of loves sweetest hugs

As we rise and make up
For time lost
Or time that shall never come
In coyness there is boldness
Amidst desire there is constraint
But love lives immortal

As the day opens up
And the hustle rushes back
We too shall start
With a glow on our face
Shining in confidence and peace
For the day shall soon close
And night will embrace us
To prove what is ours
What is gone and what is left
Time shall tick off
But the sun will remind us
That we shall glow and glitter
Throughout the day
To be together waiting for another day.

2002

Life Mid Stage

Life mid stage
Half way past
Half way ahead
This stage of life
The point of equilibrium

Life mid stage
Each with one's own lessons and values
Now shaped into the persona without paradoxes
This stage of life
The blooming is complete in its wholeness

Life mid stage
Realization of clear goals and ends
The haze is clear of all confusions
This stage of life
When the bloom is able to share its nectar

Life mid stage
Also a closure to instability of thoughts and actions

As wisdom sips into the channels of survival
The blossom too knows the limitations of period of full bloom

Life mid stage
A waiting with uncertainty and fear
As the petals will soon start to wither
The colour shall fade
The nectar will be taken
As the blossom will lose the fragrance
A journey towards an end

Life mid stage
Half way past
Half way ahead
This is the stage
Of closure of completed tasks
Of openings of preparations
A preparation of gradual withdrawal amidst the uncertain
A readiness to be able to face the unpredictable
Experience is our tutor
Wisdom is our guide
Life itself is the subject
Delicately balanced point of equilibrium.

2022

Wonderland

Many does dream of wonderland
Of fairies and angels with sparkling wands
Of elves and goblins to make the rounds
The king who rules vast and wide
Embossed in gems and golden throne
Of queens who live above all in her bed of roses
Princes and princesses whose lives are marked with fame and wealth
In abundance and bountiful lavishness

The dream of a wonderland
Is all but true
The king has fought innumerable battles inside and out
The queen has wept till her pillow soaked
Princes and princesses whose lives are dictated and toed

The life so blissful is the curtain
The scenes behind are not for all to see nor bear
The dedicated sacrifices and enduring hardships
Of body, mind and soul
Through turbulence and turmoil with toil and sweat

The dream of wonderland
Is beautiful with eyes lulled in sleepiness
When mind is at rest and the soul is in search
Where passion claims the heart's desires
And the world is blanketed in the sootheness of moonlight
The dream to be in wonderland
Be it of the king or the knight
Be it of the princess or the angel
The dream of being in wonderland.

2022

Journey

How far shall the soul travel
Dragging the body around the globe
The thirst of the soul has no limits
For the soul can absorb without saturation
The body shall tire and weaken
The ageless soul dwells in the mortal case
The case shall wither in the journey to quench the thirst

Draw your limits draw your boundaries
The point where the body shall not be dragged
Only to live in blissful solitude
The soul travels not in search of fame or wealth
The soul journeys to live in peace
The soul is immortal and so are its needs
To become a higher spiritual being.

2022

Defeated in War

At the stroke of midnight
The news lines buzz
A state under attack
Not from those afar or distant
But thy neighbor
The world awakes shaken and awed
Leaders and civilians
Men, women and young
Citizens of all color and creed
Questioning and debating
Discussing and wondering

And all these when cities were burning
People dying or are left to die
Always alert for need to act upon the sound of the siren
Hiding in bunkers and basements
As missiles destroys targets

Time when judgments of righteousness fails
For there is justification of every action

The act is situational and about that moment
Justification is in that period of performance

As the world is inhibited by those rational souls
Whose dictates decide the future of the world
There is no conqueror nor defeated
There is none who is supremely powerful
Rationality failed the essence of existentiality
Humanity is sacrificed and butchered
There is no winner
All are but defeated unilaterally against the cry of humanity.

2022

Masked Men and Veiled Women

The world is filled with masked men
And yes I put it as men
For they are one half of the rational creatures
Whose ways decide the destiny of the earth
Be it the women or the children
Be it of flora or the fauna
Be it of resources and the sources
Through domination and manipulation
Through finest sharp cuts that bleeds and aches later on
Through the cunningness and cruelty
Continuously justified and correct
Being always right and knowing
So masked are the men

The world is filled with veiled women
And yes there do exist women
Behind they toil tirelessly and timelessly
Becoming victims of use and abuse
To be moulded and shaped
Whose opinions are immaterial

Who are crowned only when the men decides
To act upon their whims and wishes
To be suppressed and oppressed
So veiled are the women

Am I biased
Am I too opinionated

The world is filled with masked men
And yes these are men again
Whose advices guide the course of women
Whose help is indispensable for the other half
Whose generosity is so heavy a burden
Whose presence is defined to become visible
Who decides and legislated the rules and laws best for alas but all
So masked are the men

The world is filled with veiled women
And yes the women if you can see beyond
Who happily submit to the always correct men
Who smile until eyes cannot hold her tears
Who silently cleans and cleanse the acts of all
While nourishes and supports in silence

Who accepts the rules and laws for there is no way out
So veiled are the women

Ohh gender equality
How could I forget
Time when women have stood up
To stand on an equal footing if not above
To cherish womenhood and mark her presence
To show that they are indispensable
To complete the puzzle
The veil shall be taken off by the masked men.

2023

All in the Moment

All I the moment
A wink
A smile
A tear
All in the moment

All in the moment'
Being alive
Just gone
An emotion
A stillness
All in the moment

All in the moment
Make a memory
Sing a song
Shake your legs
Do your will
All in the moment

All in the moment

To appreciate

To abuse

To hold on

To let go

All in the moment

All in the moment

The moment of memories

The moment of being alive

The moment being what we are born to be.

2022

Moment of Feeling Alive

Make a memory
Sing a song
While you still can pitch high and low
Shake your legs
While they are strong
Do your will
Before wishes fade away
AND
Moments turn to memories

In that moment
Before the blink can change
Appreciate
What you have while it lasts
Hold on
What is still left as bits
Let go
Of the things that never was yours
AND
Moments turn to memories

All in that moment

AND

Moments turn to memories

2022

New Age Ideology - Technologism

How smart are the smartphones
Should I ask or stay hush
Bringing together the outer yet fragmenting from within
Casting away all barriers and norms cultured through centuries of struggle
Making the private public on the largest viewership platform
Making the individual private with security within families
Autocorrecting the creator and influencing the behavioral attitude
Influencing changes very swiftly in the whole global scape
Too quick and too giving to all
Everyone knows a bit of everything around
These days thanks to the smart devices
How smart are the smartphones
One of the popular tools of the new age capitalist
No more an age of bourgeoisie and proletariat
This is an age of technological enslavement
Governed by technologism.

2022

(Technologism as a term has come naturally to my mind during the period of composition though I have never heard or read about it anywhere else. I attribute the term with the meaning – the new age capitalism, no more about bourgeoisie and proletariat but about enslaving the masses through technology)

The Maiden

A maiden waits and stares

Longingly looking ahead as the golden rays spreads with the rising sun

Watching many around – nature, man and man-made

Some investigated and some ignored

Eyes that sees beyond herself to be someone… someday… somewhere…

As she breathes in the idea and the feeling of newness into her otherwise murky mundane life

She is thinking of trying to transform and grow

To become what she wants and not be what is imposed

Or

To remain where she is for fear of risk and opposition

What will she choose

Decision is not hers alone

She is controlled – family, society and state

Is she free to choose within the radius

Is she free to choose beyond the diameter

Freedom to choose is a privilege of the few
And I know not if the maiden is amongst those few.

2022

There is No Closure

Life is short
The chapters too long
The stories are longer
The days pass as if unfinished
The nights never seems to end

Life is short
Words left unspoken
Works are unending
Some songs are never sung
Some dreams never lived

Life is
Juxtaposition of elements
Days and nights
Words and works
Where the done is what and why
Where every next is may be and but
There is no closure
As a page done unfold the next

Life is short here on earth
The journey forward has no end
The soul shall forever search
Be it in wilderness or in captivity
Be it the universe or the multiverse.

2022

An Evening

As I am sitting at my desk
The laptop turned on and I can see
Files and folders from years gone by
Containing within itself a world of mine
Not locked with passwords and security options
The laptop is latest and updated
In contrast
The user is old conservative and not tech savvy
How did I and seriously how did I actually been using that on my lap for so long
Like a delicate tech box to store all my works and more
What has technology made of me
I am not the creator but only a user
Yet it holds/contains/stores all my works for decades now
And maybe
Long after I am gone and when no one remembers
For how long.

2023

What If Not

What if not you have a job
You will not get salary
What if not you have no money
You will not be able to afford the many things
What if not you are able to buy
You will slowly die from without
What if you slowly die from without
You are scared and frightened to find this out
But is the What if Not so
I dare say no
The world without will be torn
The world within shall come in unison.

2023

A Moment Housed

As far as my vision can see
I see a wonderful life ahead
A cozy home with porch and a backyard
Where flowers adorn the pathway
The kitchen is warm
The living room full with guests
The study where children are busy
As the house glows up with lamps

As far as my ears can hear
I can listen to the soft melody
The parking of cars in the porch
The pathways marked with fairy lights
The hustle and whistle in the kitchen
The living room abuzz with chatter and laughter
The study humming in resonance
As the house dances to the rhythm

As far as my voice can reach
I call to tell and preach

The vision is so satisfying
The melody is so soothing
Is this what we call our home
Where the porch is never left alone
The pathway is marked
The kitchen is stuffed
The living room full
The study room cool
The moment is housed
That was built not browsed.

2023

Puzzle Laid to Rest

When you are tensed and worried
And your world feels like falling apart
Think of the tiniest dot
A fragment that survives in fraction
For it learned the rule of survival

Break your problem
Identify the issue
Open the scar
Find the disease
Talk about the matter
Communicate fully

With communication
Doors for solution will open
Be it a yes or no
At least you progress somewhere
Better than staying stuck midway
Chocking and suffocating in self-doubt

When the path is clear
Take a step
No matter how hard or difficult
Soon a beautiful pathway will show up
There the dots will join
The fragments will fall in place
And the puzzle will be laid to rest.

2023

Ordinarily Extraordinary

A mundane gesture
A smile – sweet or broad
A greeting – namaste or handshake
A nod of approval – eyes shut or wink
Goes unnoticed
Until one sudden day
There is no smile
There is no greeting
The nod of approval is absent
The mundane is mundane
But as a feeling of loss creeps in unknowingly
The mundane is suddenly not mundane anymore
The smile had brightened a day
The greeting had wishes for that day
The nod had approval ahead for the day
Understanding changes perception
The mundane is now a special gesture
There is nothing ordinary in being ordinary
There is always something extraordinary in being ordinary.

2023

Born Human

Feelings are deep
Feelings are tender
When you are around
Feeling surrender
Deep are emotions
Tender is love
When you are around
Feelings are natural

Emotions are contradictory
Love is altruistic
When you are around
Feelings are not sundry

Happiness in togetherness
Sadness in parting
When you are around
Feelings are appreciated

Regard for the love
Respect for the loved
When you are around
Feelings are taught

To feel is to know
The ancient law of life
To teach and to learn
To accept and to deliver
To be born human.

2007

A Flight Called Life

To see the soft glow
Is like losing oneself

To smell
Is as good as musk

To hear laughter
Is like music to the ears

To feel
Is like soothing balm

When you listen
I know not what to say

The world is vast
And people many who inhibit
But still all are alien
With an exception
And that exception is you

What you feel
Matters not to me
For somewhere in the bottom of my heart
I know
We feel alike and that you belong to me

Life is a journey
We are passengers
Who meet but with a destiny
Every relation has a meaning
Which we must be able to read
Right interpretation, right inter action
Shall fulfill the journey's mission
Shall direct the passengers to their destination.

2007

Journey of Life

The sun rises
A child is born
Every moment of life
Is a continuous growth

The rising sun is now full and bright
It is morning
Spreading a hope of life
Without any prejudices
The infant becomes an adolescent
Learns and gains knowledge of
The ways of living
The tricks of surviving

Noon approaches
The sun heat is maximized
Energy at its height
He is now a family man
Extracts from life as much as he can
Maximum functionality
With maximum efforts

The heat and the brightness
Gradually slows down
As is the pace of life
Gives us a chance to relax
A little break
To refresh

Twilight marks an end
The journey of the sun
He shall now retire
From the pressures
Of being a provider
Settled in his position

Darkness engulfs
Moon reflects
The light of the giver of life and light
He reflects the days gone by

Works that are completed
The unfinished jobs
Acts that are performed
The incomplete deliberations

Hope lies in the next generation
As the sun shall rise again
Without fail
To continue the
Journey of life.

2008

Feelings

Tomorrow and Always

As the moon hides behind the clouds
Protecting the purity
The clouds embraces the beauty
Owns and possesses
The sky is theirs
So is the night
Stars keep a watch
As the rendezvous goes on
Togetherness since time immemorial
Tomorrow and always.

2021

Yours Forever

You hold me and kissed
A moment that is eternity
Intoxicating and intriguing
Lived a life in a moment
A moment of ours
Sweetest and best
The stars watched us in the full moon night
As we mingled into oneness
What a moment
Loaded and complete
Dearly cherished
Engraved in our hearts forever.

2021

Yes! You are Gone

You are gone
Far far away
In the land of your home
As you passed
You kissed my soul
To tease and love
A moment
A lifetime
Sealed in that one union
In blessing and punishment
Your are gone
Far far away
In the land of your home.

2021

Carry Me Up to the Riverbank

Pensively and silently
A quiet life I led
In a cottage by the riverside
Until a sweet gush of wind
Opened the door
To let you in

The softness and the sweetness
Engulfed my heart and soul
No longer silent
And
Now singing all day long

Carry me as far as you can
For your arms cushion my love
But you have a path to follow
That you don't wish me along

My song shall grow silent
My love shall not be taken

So carry me along the riverbank
And leave me in the flow
To be carried into the ocean
Of eternal bliss and peace
Not to be silent again
Not to be pensive

My heart and soul shall be taken over
By the angels of time and space
For I shall mingle in the river
Where you shall leave me

I want you to carry me up to the riverbank
For I will stay
In your heart and soul
My love that is pure and sacred
I worshipped this love
For long as I breathed

Carry me up to the riverbank
And let go of me in the flow
For I shall cease as you embark
On the path you have to follow
Where you wish me not to follow

Carry me up to the riverbank

Mark an end to us

Let me go

Let me flow

Without you forever.

2022

The Universe Failed

When I was your love
I was afraid
I was unprepared
I was weak and longed for you to hold me and take me with you
Was scared to even say so to you

And now,
The hand you extend is not mine to hold
The heart that beats is not mine to behold
The watchful gaze sees past me
The mind that thinks is not of me
The longings and yearnings are not to be by my side

For now,
You belong elsewhere
I feel it in the way you touch
I feel it in the sound of your beat
I feel it in the way you gaze
I feel it in your insights
The longings and yearnings are not to be by my side

I am hurt
I am in pain
Coz I know not what to do without you again

I can't hurt you
I can't oppose you
Coz all of me is you

Now
You have a hand to hold that you can't resist
You have a heart that has found its beat
You gaze has a diameter to look for
Your mind is filled with the thought of what you proclaimed as yours
The longings and yearnings have its nested presence

Move on
In your chosen path
Turn not back to see the – what of me
For you shall not be able to unleash
I shall not be able to reach myself in you
I will be lost and finished
Trying to find the me in you
Having now surrendered my all for first and forever

I can't hold the hand

I can't hear the beat

I can't match your gaze

I can't reach your thoughts

The longings and yearnings are knotted

This time we know

We know that destiny is preordained

The universe conspires to make us meet

For the universe has failed us

As you belong elsewhere

And I shall encounter a shadow

That shall appear and reappear as the rays of life shall play upon

I can't live in a bubble of emptiness

I can wait but for whom shall I wait for

I can only love from far and away for I am forbidden beyond

We failed to paddle together

We failed to stand up to each other

We failed to be there for one another

We failed to proclaim together

We failed because we feared

We failed because we did not believe in us

It was too beautiful to be true

A match that heaven couldn't make

The universe failed us because it was afraid that we seconded their best

Together we are divine, pure and one

We are perfect with each other and for one another

2022

Being Sad

When drowned in the cradle of sadness
The pain that pinches rips the soul apart
The mind is fogged and clouded
Until the eyes rain tears
The sadness lies in the mind and the heart feels heavy
In that moment of being lost
Life starts afresh with rejuvenation and renewed zest
For life is about hope against despair
In that moment of pain
Life silently tells us to look up and smile
In that moment when end is the only way
Life shows the path as the clouded mind has poured
Pain with sadness knows no end
When in pain we know the depth of the soul
In sadness the extent of grief is known
For it is about being humane and alive.

2022

For You

Don't ask me to wait
When your scent makes me dizzy and drunk
And your soft kisses caress my lips and naked me
Don't ask me to stop
When you lift me in your arms which is my heaven
When you make me sit on your lap and it feels home
Don't ask me to wait
For I want to caress your mind
For I want to kiss your soul
Don't ask me to stop
For we have waited too long enough
For in you lies my universe
Through your vision I see my world
In your words I find solace
In your presence I feel so blessed
Don't stop me to ask
For you know better than me
I shall be with you always and forever
I am only yours

I live because you make me alive

Reciprocated

Vice-a-versa…

2022

Why Us

Waiting for you
Is so sweet
But I do not want this sweetness forever
Being with you
Is so blissful
That I just want us to be blessed

Waiting for you
Is a test of my patience
But I cannot be patient forever
Being with you
Is so fulfilling
That I just want us to be full

Waiting for you
Is so heavy
I cannot carry this for long
Being with you is so carefree
That I just want us to be happy

Together we create
A world within the universe
So small in space
Yet so big and spread
So vast and unending

How could we have lived so long
Without being around
Time has pushed us
Beyond all our limitations and inhibitions
But alas I ask my mother
Why did she
If we were to come together again
Why did she play this game
If it was that we should meet again.

2022

Failed You

Why my beloved
Why us
That we failed each other
To give happiness and joy
That we failed one another
To shield and protect
That we failed to answer
To break the silence
Love and live
To be together
I bear it upon ourselves
As we each say
Failed you.

2022

A Long Time

After a long time
I put us in words
Embossed forever
Sealed in the glue of memories
Universe cannot rip the we from us
In your embrace lies my whole world
For that is all the space I need to live
In your hands lies my happiness
For it is the only hand that I can hold on forever
In your heart only is contained my life
For my heart only beats the rhythm you play

After a long time
It's we in words
Tried and tested
From teens to twenties
In thirties, forties and more…*ties*
Overcoming a thousand barriers
Disappearing to reappear without knowing why
Leaving the trail of magic to linger

Amidst the trials and lessons of life
Breaking all inhibitions
To be where - we becomes us

After a long time
But not the last
With gratitude and appreciation
The point of exaltation is reached
It is not anymore about us
It is no more we
Finally we found us.

2022

Divine Gift - Love

Some name this dependency of emotions
Some name this insecurities of availability
Some name this jealousy of not being enough
Some name this possessiveness of body and mind
And the list is endless as it goes on and on
Until
The mind shall understand just oneness
The body shall feel the oneness
The soul shall dual in that oneness
The heart shall whisper in oneness
This
You cannot hold what is not yours
You cannot control unfolding destiny
You cannot ignore the growing emotions
You cannot let go what you believe is yours
Uniquely wrapped in mirth and mystery
A divine gift
Love.

2023

Talk to Me

Talk not to me of lore and love
For we heard the tales of dove

Talk not about the days bygone
For we were young and forlorn

Talk not to me of life
For we have been through the drive

Talk not to me of what lies ahead
For we may be by then dead

Talk to me of passion and love
For we are now ready as the dove

Talk to me about the days ahead
For we are now grown and have said

Talk to me about life
For we are now truly alive

Talk to me about it all

Tell the tales and the game of ball

The dreams we saw and the passion shared

The vision to age together that we craved

The truth that we never talked

Yet we said it all as if we have forever talked

The fact that we never met

Yet we believe that we never left.

2023

Thank God I Waited

Waiting can never be so sweet
Until those who wait for the special
In anticipation and anger
Through moments of introspection and retrospection
Between the imagination
And its realization

I have waited and waited
Waited long many years
The sun, the moon and stars are my witnesses
The sun has seen me awake in the early hours
The moon has seen me looking up as we are under the same sky
The stars added sparkle to my hopes
And then we happened

Waiting can never be so sweet
Until those who waited for the special
The anger is washed away in the very moment
The moment ends all disbelieve as a new realization dawns
Waiting so long has been so arduous

Long years of resistance to not give otherwise

But alas the wait was painfully sweetest

For we did arrive

And the wait was worthy all the while

Thank God I waited.

2023

Theft

You have stolen a piece of me
From inside my core existence
Without my knowledge and knowing
When and how only you have the answer
For it is all your doing

Sometimes when I ache to feel
The emptiness reminds me
That you have stolen a piece of me

Sometimes when I need vision to see
The blurred view reminds me
That you have stolen a piece of me

Sometimes when I concentrate to work
The focus is lost and reminds me
That you have stolen a piece of me

Sometimes in midst of hustling crowd
I feel alone and lonely which reminds me
That you have stolen a piece of me

Sometimes I do ponder and wonder
Is this act of crime or of a coward
Else that of surrender and failure

You have kept with you what is mine
Without my knowledge and knowing
Not the owner nor master but only the possessor
What you think is precious and belonging to you
But had it been yours
You wouldn't have stolen a piece of me

2023

How Can You

How and how can you
Sweetly don a smile
When your life is falling apart
And the eyes are crying dry

How and how can you
Be gentle and kind
When your life is ripped torn
And the eyes are crying dry

How and how much more to go
For the tears must flow
Let the fallen break away and be washed
Let the torn be rinsed to be rid off
And the eyes smile in gentle kindness.

2022

Craziness

Is this the craziness around
Or the craziness inside
When the world looks like a puzzle
And the earth is turning inside out
To be amazed or be amaze
The craziness is everywhere.

2022

Ode to Parents

You are the cause
Of existence

You are the source
Of affection unlimited

You are the one
Who showers love

You are the tutor
To teach the first lessons

You are the guide
In the journey of life

You are the shield
To protect from harm

Will you become the reason
For us to live.

2007

Irreparable Damage

You passed by me
Like a gust of swift wind
Strong and hitting against the rock
Leaving a crack and marking it as damaged

The wind blew away
The rock shall never know where
Only the crack is left
To widen with time
And let any wind now
Passing swiftly by
To feel the rock
As it was never able to do before.

2007

Hope

There is pleasure
In the memory
There is joy
In the past

There is pain
When unrequited and rejected
There is sorrow
In the present

There is hope
For the future
There is desire
To wait

Hope
Which only man can
With sense of fulfilment
Without ability to fulfil
With plans

With targets
With anticipation
Without assurance

Only a reflection
Not a true image
Of what we want to be
Of what we are not meant to be
Of what we can be

Reminding of our existence
As being born
Rational
With all its irrationality.

2007

The Kiss

Too long for
Is to desire
To feel
And to gather

You have left me
With a kiss
That I shall forever cherish

O my love
My passion
If I may call you so
Whence shall you
Turn around
I shall never know.

2007

Loose Love

Love that
Which is an emotion
Should be made to feel
Intensified in the absence
Of the lover
To feel so restive
For pleasure or pain
Stretching emotions
To an extreme where there is but
One feeling
Love

Love that
Which is a longing
Should not be overcome
The passion let loose
Without a lover's presence
The desire to link
The longing to embrace
Be resisted

To the point
Where there is realization
Of one sensation
Love

Love that
Which is an expression
Should be expressed
In ways subtle yet hinted
To test the strength
Of reciprocity
To understand
Longing and emotion
Whether of envy
Of love
Whether of today
Of tomorrow
Expression shall find an answer
To deepen the bond
To enjoy the feeling

To get bonded
Shall never give
The passions
To play again

To unite
Shall never give
The emotions
To shuffle again

Continuity spoils
Sweet memories
Which must always be
“”Sweet reminiscences”
Freeze at one stage
Inert and unchanging
In one lovable moment
For to possess love
Is to lose the
Value of love
The value of being in love.

2007

The Maiden Waits

The night is dark
The city is asleep
Calmness prevails
The hustle bustle is now quiet

Inside the homes
Days work done
Members are resting
Somewhere
In this quietness
In the calmness

The maiden waits
As she rests her head
In quietness
Not known to any
With dreams and
With tears in her eyes
Absorbing the stress
Of life and love

Life without love
What would she do when night befalls
And darkness surrounds

Love without life
What would that be
The night questions her
The darkness makes her contemplate

Eyes close
Without answer
As if
End of night
Will find an answer

Tomorrow
Shall decide
How to live with love

2008

If It Wasn't For You

If it wasn't for you
I would never have known
That the clouds do sing
And raindrops dance

If it wasn't for you
I would never have known
That the honeybees buzz
While the petals flutter

If it wasn't for you
I would never have known
That the river runs to mingle with the ocean
The meadows stretch to kiss the horizon

If it wasn't for you\
I would never have known
The heated play of the fire that burns
The cooling ice that calms and gives shivers

If it wasn't for you
I would never have known
That purpose of why I was born
The reason why I shall die.

2023

Lo Lo-V-ESS

Loss is grief but not so always

Loss is emptiness but not so forever

Loss is failure but not necessarily

Loss is not as conceptualised

Loss enables the ability of feeling alive

Loss is space for advent of another season

Loss is an analysis for improvising

Such is the uniqueness of loss

It oozes what is wanting to vent out from the depths of our heart

It builds stepping stones to climb up in life

It mirrors for growth and enrichment

The proportion and degree of loss is personal

The feeling added with living through it

A unique balancing of letting go yet creating what to hold on

To appreciate with gratitude what is gone

To gear up and be prepared for the advancing newness
Loss is the second heaviest emotion
Second only to love which tops the chart
LO-LO- the art of living victoriously with all ESS…

2024

Love Is Not What Is Said

For you I love but not to be lost
For you I love but not to be abused
For you I love but not to be toyed

This isn't the love you speak off
This isn't the love you make feel
This isn't the love you act upon

Once loved cannot be reloved
Once loved cannot be unloved
Love is simply love

I loved so I dare to let go of expectations
I loved so I dare to move on alone
I loved so I dare to leave with peace and simply my love.

2024

Simple Love

If love is all that love can be
I will wait for you till eternity

If love is all that love can be
I will live through infinity

Love is a natural click that stays on forever
There is no space nor gap
There is no interference nor reference
There is no proposal nor promise
There is no closure nor stop

Love is only what is between the two
It is being heard in silence
It is about feeling without being
It is about presence even in absentee
It is about mirrored identities

Love is when the heart misses a beat
Love is when loneliness grapples in a crowd

Love is becoming restless to share
Love is giving and caring

Love is also a silent retreat to let others be happy
Love is closing down to disappear and not disturb
Love is tears through heartache
Love is the only pain that time does not heal

If love is all that love can be
We will live through eternity

If love is all that love can be
We will be together for infinity.

2024

Bonfire

As the bonfire lights up the winter night
With its warmth and ember brightness
The flames engulfs the chillness and the heat from within itself
The flames bright fresh yellow and sacrificial orange hues
Suddenly a shade of sky like blue mingled in earth's affairs
As if it burns itself to let others stay worm and feel cozy inside the shawl wrap
Until it is completely burnt out and charred
The redness will soon cool down and turn to ashes
To be finished and become anew.

2024

Existence

Winter Winds

Winter winds
Blows of chillness
Windy and flurry
How far you have travelled
Never tired
Relentlessly you continue
To blow ahead
Kissing the cold landscape
Hugging beings with the feel of winter
Strange are your ways
Are you cold
For soon you shall blow away
With a sweep of chilling lushness.

2021

Summer Breeze

The wind blows
Hot and humid
As in rage to swipe away
To burn down
The race that destroys its coolness
The breeze that lost its soothing compose
It blows disturbingly
A gush of heat and humidity
Yes in rage
To swipe away
To burn down
The race that destroys its warmth.

2021

Feather Paired Souls

The feathers are lightly ruffled
Still yellow and black
Waiting in the same old tree
Stubbornly perched on the same branch

Your paired feathered soul
Is always flying alongside
You meet in the same place
Reminiscing the carefree old time
When life was free and you wanted to fly

Your paired feathered soul
Is still by your side
The two of you play in coyness
Make lasting memories

The feathers are lightly ruffled
Still yellow and black
The wait is over

Both have found your nest
In the same old tree
Happily nestled on the same branch.

2021

Come to Flow Again

Where is the water
That flowed across the valleys and hills
That told us to keep flowing
For life is never the same
Each moment brings newness
Of existence and substance

Where is the water
For the river is parched and thirsty
Its bed is bare and vulnerable
The bed is its constant home
The water may flow high or low
Elements balanced amidst the transient and the permanent

Where is the water
That flowed across the valleys and hills
Come bouncing once again
The river shall not be born

Only of the barren bed
You need to wash its woes
To make way for the bay.

2022

Mighty Ocean

The mighty ocean lies ahead
I am standing on a foot patch of sand
The expanse so vast
The stretch beyond vision
Engulfed in the mightiness of the mighty ocean
Waves repeating constantly to touch the shore
As a child runs up to touch the mother before running away soon
And the game goes on and on

The mighty ocean lies ahead
There seems no start nor end
From whence you flow to where
No one shall ever know
Absorbed in the mightiness of the mighty ocean
Whose depths holds nature's treasure
Various and innumerable from life we know not
Like a child hiding away all its possessions at impenetrable depths
Keeping them guarded and protected from harm and extinction

The mighty ocean lies ahead

Whose shore cannot be seen

Unpredictable beneath the calm stretch

Always a challenge to conquer

Sailors' dream to be in its lap yet cruise at their will

Adventurers want to explore in the excitement

Pirates and traders all wants the mighty ocean to be in their stride

The mightiness of the mighty ocean lies far and beyond

A tale in itself or is it a treasury of tales

Life lives and gets ended as the mighty ocean whims and dares

Standing on a foot patch of sand

Watching the might of the mighty ocean that lies ahead.

2022

The Ancient Verse

Ancient are the ways of life
The soil that binds is so old
The water that flows is since unknown
The air we breathe has always been
So it the verse
You and me
Amidst
The changing forms of physical existence
The soul dwells in the ancient
There is no beginning nor an end
Just the constant presence of flow and ebb
The young strong and uncertain
The old grow weak and wise
As elements collide in contrast and unison
There is no beginning nor an end
Just the constant presence of flow and ebb
As ancient as the ways of the verse.

2022

Spring

As flowers bloom and spring advents
The grounds are colourful with greener leaves and blossoms full
The humming returns to build their nests in branches and window sills
As I look around and jot a few lines
The chameleon stares from afar camouflaged and unknowing that it is seen
It moves from grass to hedge and fence to gate
Thinking itself as hiding but alas I am spotting the track
The bees buzz and wake up the flowers
To dig in the nectar of life with sweetness loaded
Creatures are now gay and joyful after the cold spells of chilliness
Spring is life at its best after harsh winter days
Spring is life at its best before the rains wash it all away

Spring is celebration
Love for life

Hope against despair
Of moments and of being
Of the beauty of the creator.

2022

Early Morning

Waking up to the bright rays of the summer morning
When the heat spreads before the rise
Activities get started early as the day rises up
But you lie lazily under the rotating blades unwilling to part with the bed
Your innocent smiles and charms
As you roll squeaky with eyes refusing to open up
You allure me to join you for together you want to start the day
With me beside you.

2022

Clouds

While flying above across many a places
The ride amongst the clouds
So soft and fluffy all in white
Nested in the bright blue sky
Delicate they appear as if cradled in the lap of nature
Up above they float in patterns of cotton fluffs
This feels like fairyland
As if they house the fairy queen
Whose castle lies in the clouds
Where angels live and call this their home
The balls of cloud each distinctive
Lined across the skyscape
So beautiful pure and serene
Like a white orchid in the spring.

2022

Path of Life

The path of life starting at birth
Destined to be walked upon
There is no escape nor reversal
Only a one directional path
Face it or fear it
Accept it or deny it
The path has to be walked upon
Crawling and climbing
Running and jogging
There is no stoppage
The map is in our palms
Directions on the forehead
The path is not endless
The path shall disappear with the last breath.

2022

Lone Magpie

Hopping from branch to branch as if in search of…
Why are you so restless even while your wings can carry you everywhere
Your chirpings are call for attention, admonition or admiration
Your feathers are not ruffled and rough
You freely roam without permission or consent
You peck and pick what you want as feed
Yet you appear restless and in search
Alas you alone a victim of omen and of hard luck'
You shall find calmness as you meet your twin flame
But for now you must search and look around for
Another lone magpie a little far away.

2022

By the Lake

From a distance I can see the lakeside slowly getting crowded
I bring the teapot to a boil as the first blue rays kisses the earth
The dawn is cracked by the chirpy birds that flies out of the nest after a rested night
There is so much silence around that I hear the water bubbling in the pot

The verandah calls me to come and sit while sipping freshly brewed tea
But my eyes are wandering and my soul is as fresh as is the day
Of all that surrounds I cannot withhold but stare at the lake below
This is not the first and definitely not the last that I am absorbed and lost by the lake

Beautifully surrounded by pathways and patches of flowerbeds
The fishes playfully swim in a swirly mood
The ducks quack

And add white elegance to the lake
The lotus blooms in a corner making the lake feel divine and blessed
The gates are closed but will soon be open for joggers and walkers
The benches have been there since long hearing the stories of love and lorn
The boats are waiting for those who would like to paddle and row

The gates have opened and the crowd comes in to start another day
For the flowers will have admirers' poets and photographers
The fishes will meet visitors new and old
The benches be now filled with people and their stories
The boats rowed around to feel the breeze passing by
The pot is empty and the rays are golden
I don't want to get going but I must
Till another pot is brewing and the verandah calling.

2022

Divine Dream

I looked around and am mystified
Is this real or in a dream
I find myself amidst beautiful greens
The pleasant wind hugs and passes by
Ancient monasteries standing tall
Sacred serene spirituality

I look around and am mystified
Is this real or in a dream
The path I follow is guided by hillsides
Until I come across a garden of kiwi vines
Tasted the fruits and the wine
So sweet and divine
Growing bountifully in the stretches of vineyards

I look round and am mystified
Is this real or in a dream
The tops are snow clad
Grounds white and pristine

What a sight…amazed and awe struck
This is nature in her purity
Wrapped in divine peace

I looked around and am mystified
Is this real or in a dream
The people so sober and nice
Bearer of their past
Accommodating the present
Moving forward towards the future
Blessed by the divinity of the land

I hear a melody
As the alarm plays soft tune
How could it be real
For I haven't been to your land
Wishfully longing to be in your lap someday
Tour the valleys and the hills
Through monasteries and kiwi vineyards
To be kissed by the soft sun
Feel welcomed by the people
Experience the melting moments amidst the snow

Lived a reality with eyes shut and mind open
A divine dream.

2022

(Published in www.matrixarunachal.wordpress.com
Matrix Anthology Vol II 2022-23)

Song of Life

Chorus alongside me
The song of life
Where butterflies spread their wings with coy
And the bees bumble and buzz with joy
Where scented flowers bloom to their full
And the fruits ripen to sweetness cool
Where birds nestle and sing their song
And the squirrels hide their nuts for long
Where children play and run along
And their pets can stay for long
Where the fireflies adorn the gardens bright
When night befalls and the moon is shining right
Be there by my side
To sing in chorus the song of life.

2023

The Dance

A swirl
A twirl
And round about
The maiden dances unaware
The flowers swing
The leaves rattle
The birds chorus
The bees drum humming
The gentle breeze
Takes a pause
Caught all by surprise
And then
The pause.

2023

Life is an Invite

Invited to be born
And the growing goes on
The lying baby is invited to crawl
Then to walk and stand tall
The years pass by through invite to study and nurture
Till the time when invited to add some structure
Invitation to get hooked
Life demands for another to be booked
A call for Life that is so glorified
Only as long as the invite has not expired.

2023

Dawn Breaking

Cloudy sky awaiting to be sunny and bright
Droopy sleepy eyes refuses to open up just like the sky
The flowers are afraid to bloom alas the petals are torn apart
The calves and chicks are kept enclosed
What if they get lost and hurt
The birds are scanty and still in hiding
But the thunder lights the sky with bolt
Showers and pours hesitantly as if wanting to withhold
Let the sun be seen when the dark clouds are gone
The sunny sky shall not take long.

2023

Immortal Feel

I promise to hold your hand
As long as I breathe and am alive
As long as my senses are knowing
To be by your side no matter what and where

The sun can only brighten our days
For the scorching rays will fail our passion
The breeze shall not shatter our home
For the gushing wind will fail to break our bond
The rain will bring us prosperity
For the downpour cannot dampen our spirit
The moon will remind us of our eternal love
As new moon shall always grow full again

As you say so I hear
As you show so I see
For there is happiness in the version of ours
For there is joy in the vision about us

This is more than a mere exchange of vows
A dedication to be together
A desire to consider and care
A feeling that is immortal…love…

2023

Flight of the Flock

You and your flock comes every year
Flying for a thousand miles
To call the wetlands your home
Build your nest and breed your brood

A fleet of flocks land
In batches of various/diverse breed/species
Who has taught them the route
I wonder year after year
Un-dauntingly precise and knowing
For months on they fly relentlessly
In search of a place they can call their nest
Towards the place they have always called their nest

A search for nest
A search so important
To be alive and breed
To enable continuity

Responsibility and responsiveness

Towards nature.

2022

(About the migratory birds that annually migrates to the Pobitora Wildlife Sanctuary, Assam, all the way from Siberia)

Space

Lying on the outdoor
A hot summer night
The full moon I so adore
The sky is bright
But my mind is drawn indoor
And feeling not so right

The sky is not the limit
The space beyond is so full of mystery
Stars shining bright as a dot
Yet they burn out and bury
Out there in that space that I cannot count
Apprehend, comprehend nor study

As a child I loved astronomy
But as I grew practicality shaped my existence
I was not allowed to learn about anatomy
It was all about prevalent societal sense

As I lie and watch the same sky that belongs to nobody
Transcendal exchange of energy through existence.

2023

Moon Landing

The moon a symbol of love relentless
The moon a symbol of passion unending
The moon a holder of the secrets of the universe
Playing in coyness amidst light and darkness

Moon's beauty is a matter of perception
Poets immerse in your fullness and glow
Scientists driven by the secrets unknown
Worshippers rever your power and sanctity

So gracefully accepted Vikram Lander in moonlap
To cradle and nourish with information
As India makes it mark in space history
To conquer the lunar south pole

The nation salutes the untiring scientists
The relentlessly working associates and agencies
A journey as difficult and as beautiful as the moon itself
Drawing strength from dark days
To rise above and be the brightest

A transition from no moon to full moon
A travel from no where to being there

A moment of applause
Cherished and engraved
In the history of space research
As men will continue to achieve further
A love for the unknown

The passion to conquer
To lay bare the secrets of the universe.

2023

Drizzling After a Long Time

It's drizzling after a long time
The parched soil is dying to quench her thirst
The earthy smell after the first few drops
No chemist can concoct
So romantic pure and heady

It has now started to rain
The fragrant earth is lost
As the thirst is quenched
Bathing every creature, plants and objects
And soon the dusty dry look is replaced
There is more greenery as the blackish brown dust is washed away
As parched barrenness is drenched

Now it's pouring like no time is left ahead
The elements are also in a hurry
To deliver and be on time

As nature charts their schedule
Without fail and without expectations.

2023

Grass Blade

The grass blade
Holds the droplets of rain
As the sun peeps through the now uncondensed clouds
The grasess are no longer standing green
But dazzling like prism and rainbow drizzled.

2023

Terrace View

The city below is a concrete jungle
As eyes try to look beyond the cemented walls
A fine line of greenery spreads
Like the horizon
When heaven bends down to kiss the earth
Men's creation can stretch that far
Where nature bends to accommodate within her
The city skyline and the high rise
The innumerable vehicles and the honking
The densely populated apartments designed to gather the crowd
Where infrastructure may fail amidst one whim of nature
To be urbanized or modernized
The choice is ours
The future is ours.

2023

Washed Away

When the clouds come pouring down
On the parched and thirsty grounds
How the earth sends its thankful gratitude
Through earthen scent waffling in the air
What a moment of aromatic perfection
As each being wants to breath in the scent
A scent short lived in time but lingers in the mind
Some rush out in the open to soak in
Some sit in the verandah and club it with chai and pakoras
Some want to sit indoors over cards and good old peg
While in the other parallel city
Some are afraid as they have always lived soaked in the open
Some are fearful as life is all about one verandah shade
Some try to grab indoor for they might otherwise loose it all
But the scent is carried away with the winds
As thunder bolts the skies and lightning strikes
The innocent aroma is lost
What started with fragrant promise
Is now washed away in the flowing flood of reality.

2023

So As To

As petal is to flower
So are my feelings
As leaf is to stem
So are my strength
As stem is to branch
So are my benchmarks
As branch is to trunk
So are my targets
As trunk is to roots
So are my roles
To maketh whole a growth
Matured and nurturing - complete and full.

2023

Will Winter Wither

The advent of autumn
And the wind changes its fervent
As nature prepares for a retreat
And the air brings a closure of sorts
Nature gears up for harsh days ahead
In anticipation and preparation
What if winter never arrives
Will winter wither…

2023

It's Autumn

Autumn mornings
The sky opens up
The sun as bright as it is meant to be
Somewhere the heat is but cooler
As I am sitting in the same old verandah
There are a few missing birds
Have they migrated ahead of winter
There are a few plants that are closing to bloom
Is it because of approaching winter
Then again few other plants that are budding after long
May be to welcome winter
The not anymore green leaves are resting on the ground
The trees look less voluminous
As they conspire with nature
To lay bare it's truth
No more leaves
No more flowers
Decorations and adorations

Replaced by emptiness

To be alone

As is said – the sun too shines alone.

2023

Highway

The drive through the highway
Opens a gateway to feeling of freedom in body and mind
Openness and unlimited expanse ahead
For where will the road lead to
Dozens and a hundred places
A long stretch of concrete in middle of nowhere yet leading somewhere
Sometimes a curve and then the shady highway
Then a up and down through hilly roads
One side blocked and another open to the gorge
Through bends and curves over plains and hills
The highway is a path open to receive
It is but for the traveler
To find one's location
As all roads will not lead to the desired destination.

2023

Almighty Sun

The rising of the sun
Is never too late
Nor early

The setting of the sun
Is never too early
Nor late

The rays gives us
Life
The rays spreads
Hope

Life given
Without calculation
Without measurement
Of profit and loss

Hope spreads
Without commitment
Without promise
Of a life that must be lead

Every living being
Waits for the sun
To rise when it is time to rise
To set when it is time to set

Round this is
Birth, growth and decay
Rotation and revolution

Each and every action
Each and every process
In the living world
Depends on the
Almighty Sun

2008

Nature

Nature is loving
Nature is cruel
Nature is our friend and foe
Nature is us
We are part of nature
Inseparable and inalienable

The first rays of sun
That spreads light and life
Shines till the moon rises
Rests till moon sets

The first blossoms
The budding flower and leaves
The chirping of the birds that sings
The cooing of the pair that swing

The first drops of rain
That touches our mind and body
Rejuvenates and relishes
Thoughts and senses

The flakes of snow
The cold gust of wind
Freezes us in time physically not spiritually
Contrasted it makes us realize the value of opposites

Each change is enjoyed and welcomed
The freshness that it brings
The contrast sharp
The adoption life

Nature is not demanding
Nature is not biased
Nature produces gives distributes
Nature is our mother.

2007

Innocence

The little bundle of joy
Unaware and unknowing
Either happy or crying
Speaks of innocence

With the sound that are not words
With expressions that are not polished
With movements that are not codified
Without learning
Without training
With naturalness
Speaks of innocence

Innocently s/he takes
Unaware of the economies
Innocently s/he gives
Unknowing of the psychologies
Speaks of innocence

No manipulation
No calculation
Sheer determination to live
Speaks of innocence
Survival of the innocent.

2007

Fire and Ice

A block of ice
A flame of fire

The ice melted faster
The heat increased it glow

Who is finished first?
The ice into water
The fire into ashes

So ice said to the fire – I will turn into water
Fire said to the ice – then the glow shall be over
Ice replied – I am liquid shall condense
Fire replied – my heat shall transform your form
We are never done.

2007

Time the Master

A thought
An expression

Is a long distance
To travel

We are in a situation
We comprehend the same
Thinking for long
And a thought is formed

Time passes
Time has neither friend nor enemy
It is its own master
Knowingly or unknowingly
We wait to express
In some way or the other
An expression takes places

Paradoxical
Our desire to find a solution
Is but framing a thought
Implementation of an expression

Time is but the Ruler
The rules have to be followed

Otherwise
Thinking is wrong
Expression is futile.

2008

Seasons of Love

Oh the one
You make me wait
Testing endurance and continuity
I will stay for reasons
I can
Endure and continue
Receive and reciprocate

We meet in spring
And flowers blossom
Life is fresher
The cool breeze sweep across
Birds humming and chirping
As if consenting
Our destiny
To concile and transform
As one being

Approaching summer
Maturity and advancement

The hot air surrounds
New flocks of birds are added
The one being
Has come a long way
Waited and courted
Continued and matured
Reconcile and accomplished
Destiny as destined
To be

Autumn brings a windfall
It is time to shed
Preserve and conserve
Nothing new
But gathering all that is left
Of spring and summer
The one being
Will we fall apart
Breaking hearts
Shattering souls
Destiny shall show again as if
Not to be

Destined or not destined
Will we pass through

Through the winter of our lives
Warming against the bitter cold
Enduring together with unification
To be part of each other
Come what season may
Come what destiny say
Comes only what we wish for ourselves
As one being

Season soon changes
Winter to spring
Cycle continues
Last season's foliage
Is thicker and greener
Flocks have arrived
Adding newer music
Everything continues
As if
Summer has taught
Fulfillment of efforts
Autumn has taught
Endurance through time
Winter has taught
Togetherness though hardship
And a beautiful vision

Of hope that never dies
Of love that never fails
Of destinies that meet but once
Never to fall apart
To be for ever
One being.

2008

Winter Narrations

As the winter narrations starts with the falling leaves and withering flowers

Can I say that winter is not too far yet not arrived

The way nature prepares to welcome winter is an alarm

For man has other plans to do or dare if I may say

The acts of development versus sustainability as fact versus fake

Actions of economic progress versus exploiting nature as truth versus justification

It's human versus others

Rationality versus the irrationality naturally rational

As the lines are jotted I am not feeling the coldness of winter winds

Though the flowers are withering and dry dust coats the leaves and branches

Thinking of winter I shiver down with a spine chilliness and goosebumps

Winter that is not far yet not arrived.

2023

Temporality of Existence

As the petals open to rays of the sun
So the child gets excited near the mother
It is not planned and there is no intention
A natural conspiracy of bonding and union
This is how it's always been and always will be

The passing breeze brushes the soul
The raindrops mingles with the earth
The movement is brought to a halt
As they meet with their end of existence
This is how it's always been and always will be

The river will mingle into the ocean and cease to be
The horizon shall reach out to the sky and cease to be
The flower will bloom but no further
The child will outgrow and transform
The breeze will slow down to nothing
The raindrops will be absorbed and disappear
So are the ways of nature in transient
The now will be gone and replaced

The end will soon be another beginning
The beauty lies in between and during the phases
Everything else becomes irrelevant and necessary
All about temporality amidst the ever changing complexities.

2024

Generation Apart

Don't blame others for the hot winter and cold emotions
Don't blame others for loveless marriages and romantic affairs
Don't blame others for mobile addictions and drug abuse
Don't blame others for the rainless monsoon and parched summers
Don't blame others for species extinction and aromaless platters
Don't blame others for being alienated in a world which is growing smaller

Blame yourself for you are that generation of mankind
A generation that has threatened earth's being
Whose ambitious selfishness is camouflaged as development and progress
Whose intelligence is overtaken by Frankenstein named AI

Will we ever see hot summers and cold winters
Will we ever live lasting marriages and flirty affairs
Will we ever find addiction free and eradication of drug abuse
Will we see rainy monsoons and ponds and puddles

Will we hear the singing birds and smell the aroma of
what's cooking

May be is a word with little hope against may not
But we live only with hope and that's all we are true to
Let's hope
May the mistakes of my generation be reversed by the next.

2024

Field by the Horizon

The fields are near
The kissing horizon is but far away
Run and reach the fields
To be welcomed in the warm embrace of full harvest
Run and reach the horizon
It will but shy away and move further to become unreachable
The fields but allows itself to be kissed
By the playful horizon
To cheat and game
For nature is the playground of games.

2022

Symphony

Who has asked the sun to rise
Yet it does and shines so bright

Who has asked the moon to rise
Yet it does and continues to surprise

Who instructs the fishes to swim
And the mammals to walk
And the flowers to bloom the birds to sing
And the thunder to pour

Who has created the methods of thoughts
And the ways of expression and feeling
The momentum and movement
Of precision and timing
Who has done all these doing

It is you and me
It is us and them

The symphony of elements

The core of creation.

2023

Ethereal

Salvation

How much you are missed
Do you really want to hear
Do you really care to know
You are the wind that blows past like a hurricane
You are the water that gushes during flood
You are the fire that burns stretches of wilderness
You are the soil that buries the dead
You are the space that has become polluted
You lack courage and you are afraid
You lack strength and have no confidence
You don't deserve what you wish
You are about yourself
Reflection of selfishness and greed
You are missed
For herein lies your salvation
Not in yourself but in its reflection upon myself.

2022

Uncertainly Certain

Certainities in the uncertain word
Peace in the enraged engaged world
Food in the starved poverty stricken places
Water in parched and drought lands
Clean air in polluted zones
Happiness when yearnings never end
Mankind missed the point
Of what we want and what we need
Of desires and dreams
Of what we could have made of the world
Of what we have actually made it today
Certainites in the uncertain world.

2022

Ancient Soul

Whence you come
To where you go
We shall never know
The ancient soul
Always in transition
Moving from one to another
Seeing the verse since ages
Never repeating the sameness in life
Every birth and every stage brings newness
Your existence made possible in immortality.

2022

Always Around

I looked for you up above
In the new morning sunlit sky
In the starry moonlit night
In the heavy cloudy sky that seems to hide a tale
Where are you if not in your heavenly abode
When do I see you appear
Is it at dawn when the world is half asleep
In twilight when the world is half unseen
How do I reach you so high up above

I wish like a stubborn child to find you in your abode
Dreaming of a perfected divine floating temple
To be able to feel your presence in your brace
To be consoled by your soft voice which will show the path
To see what it is to be immortal, omnipresent and omnipotent

And then
One day spontaneously
I looked not for you up above
But I looked around me

And what a wonder it was

The sky was opening up with clouds laced with sun rays

The cock was crowing and the old man was snoring

The blooming buds smilingly looked at me

While the tired watchman fell asleep

And all I did was look around me

Realization struck and my mind was freed of presumptions

All the while you were around me immortal in the continuous acts of nature and nurture

All the while you were around me omnipresent though your creatures and creations

All the while you were around me omnipotent in the existence of life itself

I no more look for you up above

For around me you exist in very soul that breathes

For you have always been around

I feel so blessed

For you have always been around.

2022

Ageless Soul

Play not with lives
As they are souls
Play not with beings
For they are souls

The body heals
Not the soul
The body shall recover
The soul will transcend

The body can be captured to enthrall the victors
The body can be used and abused by the victors
The body endures till it perishes

The soul cannot be captured to use for enthralling
The soul liberates through transformation in transition
The soul lives on beyond the captivity of the bodily existence

Existentiality through ages
Existence defined before time.

2022

You and Me

You are the feel of soft winter snow
You are the feel of sweet autumn breeze
You are the wetness of monsoon downpours
You are the stickiness of summer days
You are every season with plenty of reasons
You are the being of existentiality
The presence in every absentee
The soul where life ceases
You are yourself of rationality and beyond
Yes it is You
The You I speak to in moments of lonely solitude
The You I look around for when in midst of groups and crowds
The You I hear when seeking answers
The You I feel with every breath that keeps me alive
The you in me and the me in you
Divinely blended for eternity.

2023

Song of the Soul

Why does the mind wonder
When the heart already knows
The brain storms to ponder
Fragmenting to understand the rhyming beats

Synchronized existence within
Contradicted and countered
Time and time again
Until the frictions brings fractions of clarity
Of thoughts, feeling and decision

Mind that delves within
While the brain is unclouded
No more deviations
No more doubts
Clarity of the rhythm
The soul that sings its song.

2022

The Traveler

What defines
The distance or the destination
The company or oneself/ be with oneself
Newer places in unknown lands
Fresh faces of people from different lands

Going and growing
Learning through sojourns
Experiencing life
Living the moments with vivid captiveness

In search of newness
Longing to unfold unknown/unread/unseen pages
To see what is already know
To find what is yet unknown

One takes a flight
Rides a train
Drives all the way
Yet

Some travel without movement
In imagination and conceptualization

Which is fairer
To visit or not to visit
To travel or just imagine
For the body is bound by compulsions
The mind is free and untiring

What defines
Destination covering a distance
In company of others or self
Newness, freshness and revisions.

2023

Bit by Bit is Lost

A bit of us is left behind
With the passing of every second
Be it of mind or of matter
Be it of being or of living

A bit of us is left behind
With the passage of every day
A memory is made
A day written off as past

A bit of us is left behind
With the adding years to our age
A stage is past experience
A newer phase awaiting with eagerness

A bit of us is created
With the time that is washed away
As we say

Life has been built

Dreams have been fulfilled/ dreams turned into reality

Goals has been achieved/reached

Between the tug of building, rebuilding and losing/ between the tug of past and future

Bit by bit of everything

It is but all lost

When it's time to call

A life is lived and nailed.

2023

Who Will Sing My Song

Should my legacy fails
And my song goes down
I will not know
Who will sing my song

In the absence of view
In the darkness of night
A lonely girl
Starting to snivel amidst her humming
Shall remember my song

In the absence of stillness
When life shall put her down
When tears shall flow on its own
She will be heard
By the silent dawn in the silent hours
She will sniffle and snuffle
Trying to sing my song

Should my legacy fails
And my songs go down
I will not know
Who will be singing this song.

2023

Sawan

An auspicious month
The trident held upright as the Ganges flow from his jata
The tilak marked as the snake wraps around his neck
The damru and
Little things I can put in the collage
For my humble existence cannot comprehend the vastness

Symbols of civilization rooted in believe of the Supreme
Mount Kailash stands tall in testimony
Unconquered by mortal beings
While the lingam is worshipped
Abhishek with water, mik
Wood apple leaves and bhang patta
Marigold and dhotura
To mention a few if not all
My fingers shake
As I struggle to capture the energy
Cage it in few words
But devotion to acknowledge

Provides me strength

The blessings shapes the verse.

(Sawan, a month in the Hindu calendar during which period Lord Shiva is especially worshipped.

Jata, is the matted hair of Lord Shiva

Damru, instrument of Lord Shiva)

2023

Who Am I

I am a writer
I know no borders
I know no boundaries

Maps cannot restrict me
Countries cannot cage me
The globe is my world

I am a writer
Imagination crosses and walks over borders
Emotions trample and stumble upon boundaries

Maps are frames of culture to be nurtured
Countries are names of entities to be understood
The globe is my world

I am a writer
My ink spills all over
My words and phrases jumps across the fence

My ideas and ideals are humane and universal
The world is my globe.

2023

Holy Ganges

On the banks of the holy Ganges
I stand to bear witness
Of events and activities
The river is made to bear upon herself

We call the river our mother
And likewise burden her with all our woes
Also sharing our wishes and achievements
In forms of prayers offerings and utmost devotion

We call the river our mother
Did we ask what woes her
Did we bother to find what makes her pleased
Like a child we just keep doing what we think best

We call the river our mother
Is it because we pray to her with believe and trust
Is it because we offer her with faith and conviction
Is it because we worship her with devotion and dedication
Is it because she accepts us without doubts and questions

Can it be not that she is giving in her totality
Can it be not that she is unfailing in her perseverance
Can it be not that she is accepting with all our flaws

On the banks of the holy Ganges
I stand to bear witness
She is a mother without bias and preferences
She is a mother to all who comes to surrender to her
She is the nurturer of our strength
She is the bearer of our civilization
Mother of all ages and sages.

2023

(The river Ganges/Ganga is considered as a holy river by the followers of Hinduism as addressed as mother/ma)

Existence

In the depth of your soul
My love is rested
Like a pearl pure and pristine

In the corner of your mind
My love is settled
Like the roots of an ancient tree

In the beats of your heart
My beats are mingled with every breath
Like a humming bird whose hum never ceases

In the existence of your being
My existence exists without any doing
Like the breeze in the wind
Like water of the river
Like clouds in the sky
Like soil in the earth
Like heat in the sun
Existence has mingled without intention

Oneness has come into being without deliberation

So we each exists.

2023

Soul

This is the direction that I have drawn for you to follow

This is the path that have to be walked upon

This is the bridge that shall drive you to me

There is no other way to reach me other than the one I dictate

I am the divinity
I am eternity
I am infinite
I am the Supreme

You have to strife through hardship and hurdles
You have to persevere through pain and endurance
You have to serve through thoughts words and work
You have to sacrifice selflessly and willingly
Above all you have to love other selves and yourself

Divinity is in the purity of each soul
Eternity is the immortality of the soul
Infinite is the soul
Supreme is the soul.

2023

In Prayer

In prayer you shall find your faith
In silence the path will be shown
Meditate pensively for the world to open up with you

In prayer you shall find your religion
That teaches about equality and humanity
Reflect in action and the world will open up in oneness

In prayer you shall find your peace
For the mind will be taught to rest
There is actually no stress that cannot be tamed

In prayer you shall find liberation and freedom
Liberation from the demeaning and derogatory thoughts and acts
Freedom from desire and want
Liberation from the baggage of physical beingness
Freedom of the soul towards spirituality.

2022

Look Smilingly and Hold Her Hand

The smile that tells me to wait beside
Not to go far nor behind
But stay alongside today and tomorrows
The hand is held tightly locked
Leaving no gap for a spike of dust
The voice curls up my existence as belonging
Not in another place or space
But in the same twirl of life together
Engulfing completely without any space for the waves to enter
The look that solidifies my stand as yours
As the moment of heartfelt waiting is over forever
The gap has disappeared in the blends of oneness
The space has merged through erased egoism as oneness defines
The moment is undoubtedly our future
The smiling look that holds the hand is the ruler of the heart.

2022

Once Again

And once
Once again
Life springs up
In lands abandoned
By men who built but lived not
Men with his ambitious heart
A crafting and calculating mind
Plotting and jotting hands
Achieves the limits of a mortal life
Through sweat and tears
Through laughter and applause
With a smile that belies
To abandon at the end
For the journey next
And once
Once again
Demand nothing but the soul.

2022

Remember

When the world falls apart
Between me and you
You feel
The sky will disappear
You feel
The sun shall not rise
You feel
The light is gone
You feel
The ground beneath is no more

Think
Of me
And
Of me

I shall make the sky appear
I shall ask the sun to rise
I shall bring back the light
I shall built the ground beneath

For you

And

For you

And the world shall never fall apart

For you and me.

2008

Our self N Other self

Life is one
It is how we live
For our-self
Or
For other-self

Birth happened
New life started
Outside
Other-self

Our-self
Had already started within
Our-self
Before birth happened

Always in life
We live
Sometimes
For our-self

Then

For

Other-self

Continuously so

Giving rise to

Situations that must be faced

Relations that must be balanced

Circumstances those are forgot or resolved

Emotions that are hated or loved

Death occurs

Self remains

Not for our-self

Or

For other –self

But

To re appear

Again

Within other-self

And be our-self

2008

Never Like This

It was never
Like this
So sweet
Even in pain

It is
Like this
So fulfilling
Even in worship

It will be
Like this
So forever
Even when
The worshipped
The worshipper
Is lost in time.

2007

Duality

In the duality of life
We survive
Changing many a roles

In every day of our living
In every phase of our growing

Through sunlight and moonlight
Through spring and summer
Through autumn and winter
Through rotation and revolution

Whether we are happy
Whether sad
Whether we are free
Whether we are bonded

Life continues
We accept the phases

As times good or bad
As ability of strength and weakness

In comparison
In contrast
What is apparent
Is the duality

Existence challenged
By opposites

AGAIN

To live
And let live.

2008

Celebration of Life

The color of life
Is the color of joy

A celebration
A call that life exist

Beyond the trivialities
Beyond snuffle and sufferings
Beyond the bondages of any control – man or material

The spreads of colors
The splash of water

Reminds us the ancient law
Of survival
The unexplainable creation of Yours
That life is a gift
Life is colourful
Life is more than
A relation between man and material

But to lead this life
Relation has to be determined
Between man and material
So that
The brightest colors glow
And Your gift
Is not dissipated
Life is but one life worth lived.

2008

Shall Wait

I shall wait for you
For period indefinite
In hope
With anticipation
In solitude
With love

Shall you ever come
I know not
But the pain
Is sweet
And so are you

Tenderness and temperament
A unique blend
Shall rule my heart
And life
If I shall have one
That I can call mine.

2008

I Am Me

I cannot read the scriptures nor the manuscripts
I cannot comprehend the writings of scholars and sages
I cannot appreciate the critics of art and literature
I am but just a simple soul
Who lives through experiences and emotions
Who lives through discussions and discourses
Who lives through words and sentences
My humble being is without shields and barriers
For I am neither above nor below
But am one with everyone everywhere.

2024

Existence Disillusioned

One who stands tall today
The one who graces the triumphant moments
Is all but a mere maya
The standing is not to last forever
The moments will be washed away in the tide of time
Maya it is
The illusion of happening and being
The feeling of presence and existence
The assertion of definiteness and truthfulness
What if the bubble bursts and things fall apart
Disillusionment – what a blissful state of being existent.

2024

Deepawali In Dilemma

As the houses and spaces light up
Gearing up to the advent of transition
From autumn to winter
In spirit of the festival of lights
In the brightness and glow
Of diyas and lamps
The oil is burnt and power consumed
The toil and turmoil id hidden if not lost in the glow of the brightened hours
The shower of sparkles after the fireworks light up a new moon night
Light and life in the darkest hour

Should I hold tight the traditions of religion and rituals
Give myself the liberty to pray and play
Through ceremonies and crackers
Should I break free from the bondages to care for the silent world
Where the nocturnal needs protection
And the animals and plants need concern and care
What is liberty – to be able to hang on or move on

Where is my freedom – who is going to untie the ties of ages
It is indeed a doubtful dilemma
Should I do
Should I abstain
If I do that what should I do
Pry to the holy Mother and play carefree
Or
Concern and act in the idea of green Diwali caring for those in waiting
Amidst all these and more
That lines cannot withhold
I do light the diya and let the oil burn
I still buy a pack of green crackers to make some noise and create the sparkle
I even go to the temple of Goddess Kamakhya
To give offerings and seek blessings
There is no doubt nor dilemma
She shows me a path that I need to follow
Peacefully pray through your play
Carefully express concern throughout the way.

2023

Being

A thought in the mind
Is but a desire of the heart
Which burdens the body
To act upon and attain
Achievement in worldly ways
Is an answer to the call of birth
So things happen within and without us
It is not to blame the mind
Nor make the heart feel heavy
But exhaust the body
For it is all in unison
One element provoking the other
To create illusion of being.

2024

About the Author

Anamika Mitra, a gold medallist in Political Science and a law graduate has experiences as lawyer, lecturer and writer (academic and non-academic), An entrepreneur hailing from the northeastern city of Guwahati in the picturesque state of Assam, she has travelled extensively across the world since a very tender age. An avid reader, swimmer, and traveller, she is self-taught in sketches and culinary innovations alongside creative writing, especially in the form of poetry. Having spent many years outside Guwahati has given her an insight on the vastness of space and the limitations of time. The exposure to multiple tiny experiences that are otherwise personally emotional has been translated in various forms of expressions. Having already published Folks of Nature – Collection of Poems, this second collection of poems ILLUSION OF BEING is a continuation of the journey already started. Currently, she lives in Guwahati and communicates through her esteemed readers via whatsapp #94355-55836 or via email: mitra18anamika@gmail.com.

www.ingramcontent.com/pod-product-compliance
Lightning Source LLC
LaVergne TN
LVHW041025150826
845672LV00001B/207

* 9 7 9 8 8 9 6 3 2 4 0 3 4 *